Columbia University

Contributions to Education

Teachers College Series

No. 352

AMS PRESS
NEW YORK

SOME RELATIONSHIPS EXISTING IN SCHOOL EXPENDITURE AMONG FLORIDA COUNTIES

BY

CHARLES ALONZO SMITH, Ph.D.

144833

TEACHERS COLLEGE, COLUMBIA UNIVERSITY
CONTRIBUTIONS TO EDUCATION, No. 352

BUREAU OF PUBLICATIONS
Teachers College, Columbia University
NEW YORK CITY
1929

Library of Congress Cataloging in Publication Data

Smith, Charles Alonzo, 1895-
  Some relationships existing in school expenditure
among Florida counties.

  Reprint of the 1929 ed., issued in series: Teachers
College, Columbia University. Contributions to edu-
cation, no. 352.
  Originally presented as the author's thesis, Columbia.
  Bibliography: p.
  1. Education--Florida--Finance. 2. Florida--
Economic conditions. I. Title. II. Series: Columbia
University. Teachers College. Contributions to edu-
cation, no. 352.
LB2826.F6S6 1972   379'.122'09759   72-177776
ISBN 0-404-55352-4

Reprinted by Special Arrangement with Teachers
College Press, New York, New York

From the edition of 1929, New York
First AMS edition published in 1972
Manufactured in the United States

AMS PRESS, INC.
NEW YORK, N. Y.   10003

ACKNOWLEDGMENTS

The author desires to acknowledge his indebtedness to Professor Carter Alexander for first suggesting the problem and for his constant assistance and encouragement during the prosecution of this study. He is grateful to Professors N. L. Engelhardt and J. R. McGaughy for their inspiration and criticisms at all times. To Superintendent W. S. Cawthon and his staff of helpers in the State Department of Education, Florida, he wishes to acknowledge his indebtedness for helpful coöperation in securing the data.

C.A.S.

CONTENTS

Contents

TABLES

SOME RELATIONSHIPS EXISTING IN SCHOOL EXPENDITURE AMONG FLORIDA COUNTIES

CHAPTER I

THE PROBLEM

INTRODUCTION

Variation is characteristic of every thriving social enterprise. Its causes may be sought in the composition of the society and in the nature of the enterprise. The causes may differ according to the time, the place, and the circumstances. Schools are normal in these respects. Since schools differ, the amounts expended for their maintenance may also be expected to vary.

Numerous studies have been made showing varying degrees of wide variation in the amounts expended per pupil for different educational functions. Many reasons for variation have been advanced by writers who have studied different school units. The need for knowledge concerning these relationships is recognized by every student of the problem.

Geographical areas have been studied and the result has disclosed wide variation in the amount expended per pupil, and relationships have been pointed out which indicate causes for these differences. States have been compared and similar conditions have been found to exist. Comparisons of cities of the same or different states have disclosed variations of like proportion. In each case, causes of the variation have been indicated. An analysis of all the units of one state with reference to variation and its relation to school conditions should prove of value.

In the discussion of relationships found in this study, certain terms will be used with a limited meaning. It will clarify the discussion from this point to define these terms now.

By *variation* we mean difference in amount paid by boards of education per pupil in average daily attendance.

Current expense is the total amount of money paid out for

1

general control, instructional service, auxiliary agencies, operation and maintenance of plant, and fixed charges.

Debt service is the amount spent in payment of bonds and all interest charges.

Capital outlay represents the expenditures for land, buildings, and equipment.

Other terms will be defined as they are used.

STATEMENT OF THE PROBLEM

This study is an attempt to analyze the current expenditures as reported in the unpublished data from the State Superintendent of Public Instruction, Florida, for 1926-27. The analysis has two purposes:

1. It will show the existing degree of variation in per-pupil expenditures for current expense among Florida counties.

2. It will determine the relationships which indicate the causes of such variation.

ANALYSIS OF THE PROBLEM

A number of questions arise in connection with this problem, two of which are concerned with variation.

1. What is the degree of variation in expenditures per pupil for current expense among Florida counties?

2. What differences are there in the unit cost for functions of which current expense is composed?

Of the questions which are related to variation, the two following are most pertinent:

1. What are the factors related to variation over which a board of education may exercise control?

2. What are the factors related to variation over which a board of education may not exercise control?

Variations in per-pupil school expenditures may be related to internal factors, or those over which a board exercises control. The policies of the board of education and the conditions over which they have control affect the amount which is expended per pupil. In this study, the counties of Florida will be compared with regard to six of these internal conditions:

1. Length of term.
2. Size of school.
3. Size of classes.

4. Degree of consolidation.

5. Per cent of indebtedness and amount paid for debt service.

6. Capital outlay.

But a board of education is influenced, directly or indirectly, in formulating its policies by external factors over which it has no control. Such conditions exist because of natural environment and resources, and the use which is made of them. A board of education, naturally, can have no control over such factors as type of population, amount of wealth, density of population, and ratio of adults to children, number of districts within a county, or the size of the county. An attempt will be made in this study to discover the relationships between these factors and the amount paid per pupil for current expense.

In order to determine from these external relationships which of these factors, if any, influence the board of education in its work, the counties of Florida will be compared with regard to the following:

1. Type of population.

2. Wealth.

3. Density of population.

4. Size and division of county.

A review of some significant studies of variation in school expenditures will aid in presenting this problem. Many such studies have been made. A few which are pertinent are reviewed here.

HISTORICAL BACKGROUND

Recent school surveys [1,2] have discussed the causes of variation in school expenditures from year to year. They have shown these variations to exist: first, in relation to the changing value of the dollar; second, in relation to an increasing number of pupils, especially in high schools; and third, in relation to a difference in the quality of the educational offering.

The amount of school service of a given quality which can be purchased for a dollar varies from year to year. It is a well-known fact that the purchasing power of the dollar has diminished during the past decade. In order to maintain educational standards which have already been established, boards of educa-

[1] *Report of the Survey of the Schools of Port Arthur, Texas, 1925-1926.*

[2] *Report of the Survey of the Schools of Lynn, Massachusetts, 1927.*

tion have been compelled to increase their expenditures. Depreciation in the value of the dollar has thus been shown by the school surveys to account for increase in the educational expenditures.

Educational opportunity for the greater numbers of pupils tends to increase the total amount of money spent from one year to the next. As the school population increases from year to year the cost of a given educational program may be expected to increase.

School surveys have assumed that better trained teachers, additional years of secondary education with more elective subjects and with more and better physical equipment meant increased quality and quantity of the education offered. Such improvements cost the board of education more money and are therefore related to variation in school expenditures from year to year.

Any study of the trends of school expenditures would be inadequate which did not consider the fluctuations in the value of the dollar. These fluctuations have been discussed in the Research Bulletins of the National Education Association which have dealt with the subject. In one of these it is stated that

> The whole truth is that a number of factors have contributed to the increase in school costs stated in dollars. The depreciation of the dollar, however, is the main factor, all the others being minor.[3]

Teachers' salaries tend to increase as the purchasing power of the dollar decreases.[4] This naturally affects the per-pupil cost.

On the other hand, variation in school expenditures per pupil for the same year, among different systems, is usually assumed to be due to other factors than the changing value of the dollar. Under such conditions, the value of the dollar is assumed to be equalized. While this is true only in part,[5, 6] the assumption serves as a working basis. Hence, conditions related to variation operating within the year must of necessity be different from those operating over a series of years. Variation here does not apply to a changing value of the dollar. We are here con-

[3] *Research Bulletin of the National Education Association.* Vol. I, No. 9, March, 1923, p. 75.

[4] Burgess, Randolph, *Trend of School Costs,* 56-64.

[5] *The Cost of Living in the United States,* National Industrial Conference Board, New York City, 1925.

[6] Norton, J. K., *Ability of States to Support Education.* Research Bulletin of the National Education Association, Vol. IV, No. 1, p. 68.

cerned with the question—What are the conditions which, in different school systems, are related to different amounts of money per unit of similar service during a year?

The manager of schools may know how expense in his system differs from the normal standard, and, if not normal, why it is above or below.[7]

It is evident that at the same time it was thought by some that variation in the amount expended could be controlled and standardized. It may be inferred that it was thought that a standard price for specified educational service could and should be established.

In 1905 Dr. George D. Strayer classified the expenditures of fifty-eight cities under nine different heads with many subheads. When compared,

. . . the most striking thing to be noticed is the variability which exists among cities. . . . As a matter of fact, we find a great variability in total amount per pupil spent, as well as in the amount spent for the various items. No one believes that the city which spends $54.00 per pupil furnishes an education six and three-quarters times as good as the city which spends only $8.00 per pupil. On the other hand, it hardly seems possible that the opportunity for education in the eight dollar city can be equal to that found in the fifty-four dollar city.[8]

Of the conditions related to variation he has this to say:

. . . either the teachers receive a very much smaller salary in the cities which pay a relatively small amount per pupil, or they have much larger classes to instruct, or both conditions taken together explain the variability.[9]

Although Dr. Strayer is not discussing causes, he points out vital factors which affect varying amounts spent for each pupil.

At about the same time, W. H. Harris, United States Commissioner of Education, made a study of school costs in which he grouped the states geographically and compared the groups. After showing the wealth and earnings of the states and groups, he showed that the total current expenditures and the amounts paid for salaries varied as the wealth of the sections varied. The more wealthy states spent more money per unit, for example:

The total amount expended for schools on an average for the whole nation is $11.17 for each person five to eighteen years of age, and $11.32

[7] *Proceedings of the National Education Association*, p. 345, 1899.
[8] Strayer, George D., *City School Expenditures*, p. 104.
[9] *Ibid.*, p. 53.

for each adult male. In the North Atlantic division the amount raised for each person between five and eighteen years of age is $18.13. The amount for each person of school age in the South Atlantic Division is $4.18 and the amount per adult male is $5.56. The amount raised in the South Central Division is only $3.94 for each person of school age. The amount for each person of school age in the North Central Division is $12.75. The Western Division in its amount per individual of school age exceeds that of the North Atlantic, being $20.16 for each person.[10]

The variation for states shown in this study is similar to that reported by Dr. Strayer.

Commissioner Harris says of causes of variation:

> The less received from taxation at a given rate for public expenses— say school expenditures—the more the individual must pay from his own earnings.

He indicates that as the southern states increase their earning capacity, their expenditures will compare more favorably with those of the more wealthy northern and western groups. From this it may be inferred that Commissioner Harris was of the opinion that ability to pay is a reason for expending more money.

On the other hand, in a study of school costs made of the states thirteen years later, Dr. Leonard P. Ayres points out that the amount which a system will spend per unit is due to aspirations and ideals even more than to wealth:

> All these facts tend to indicate that the educational effort of a state is dependent on its aspirations and ideals in even greater measure than on its financial resources. The handicap of restricted resources is relative rather than absolute.[11]

While the degree of variation shown in these two studies of states is similar, the conclusions drawn from them as to causes are contradictory. Both points of view find support by later students of the problem.

Probably the most exhaustive study of this problem was made in 1921-24 in a report reviewed and presented by the Educational Finance Inquiry Commission under the auspices of the American Council of Education. Four representative states— California, Iowa, Illinois, and New York—constituted the fields for the study. Every phase of school expenditure came under observation. Schools of the same type were compared. Schools

[10] Harris, W. H., Conditions Which Cause Variation in the Rate of School Expenditures, *Proceedings of Department of Superintendence*, pp. 53-54.

[11] Ayres, Leonard P., *An Index of State School Systems*, p. 40.

of different types were compared. Communities were selected for study. Rural territory was brought under the scrutiny of the expert's eye. Teachers' salaries were studied. Bonds and buildings were considered from the standpoint of their relations to school finance. A number of findings were crystallized in these problems.

One characteristic was common to all—variation. The degree of variation within each type and among the types is in surprising agreement. And, furthermore, it is in agreement with findings previously mentioned. The following excerpts indicate that wide differences exist in the amount of money paid per unit by different types of cities. Furthermore, it is evident that variation within a single type is greater than it is among different types of cities, as the following quotation shows:

Costs in first-class cities tend to run higher than in smaller cities. For the year 1921, for example, the average of first-class cities is $13 above that of second-class cities, and $23 above that of third-class cities. It is interesting to note that the most expensive and the least expensive city, in the state in each of the three years, were both cities of the third class.

The current expenses of elementary schools in the larger villages were even more variable than among the cities of the state. . . . It will be observed that the village average for 1921 ($66) is considerably lower than the city average for that year ($94). Although particular instances are not lacking of villages which spent more than the most expensive city, no village of this size for 1921 had as low a cost as the least expensive city.[12]

These findings are corroborated by Stoops.[13] He reports a variation for elementary schools in New York which is not so wide as it is among other groups reported. But, when expenditures of cities classified according to size are compared, variation as high as 13 to 1 is reported within a single group.

Reeves[14] found variation as wide as $121 to $38. This degree of variance is not so wide as that reported by Stoops. But, even so, it represents expenditures in one system more than three times as great as in another.

The findings in Iowa were so nearly identical with those reported in New York State that it would be possible to exchange descriptions without unduly modifying either. The Iowa study shows that

[12] Strayer, George D. and Haig, R. M., *The Financing of Education in the State of New York*, p. 45.

[13] Stoops, R. O., *Elementary School Costs in the State of New York*, pp. 18-25.

[14] Reeves, Floyd W., *The Political Unit of Public School Finance in Illinois*, p. 104.

The average cost in the first-class cities is higher each year than in the second-class cities. . . . It is worthy of note that in each of the four years the highest and lowest costs were among the second-class cities. . . . There is not a first- or a second-class city that has a cost as high as the highest approved school or as low as the lowest approved school. For city schools the widest variation is from $148 to $30; for approved schools it is from $198 to $20.

The outstanding feature of the study of elementary school costs is the wide variation, not only between schools of different types but more particularly between schools of the same type.[15]

The degree of variation in per-pupil expenditures reported for California is surprisingly great. Cost per pupil in average daily attendance varied as much as $1,481 to $33—a ratio of 45 to 1 —in California in 1921-22. Of the variations, the authors say:

The cost varies inversely with the size of the school . . . the smaller the school, the wider this variation.[16]

And again,

The cost per teacher varies directly with the size of the school. . . . The cost per teacher varies directly with cost per pupil in larger but not in the smaller schools.[17]

The degree of variation here reported is greater than that reported in other studies. The causes suggested are very similar.

Another study of school costs which has had wide influence on subsequent practice was made in 1922 by Dr. J. K. Norton. In so far as his study shows variation in per-pupil school expenditures, it agrees with former studies. He reports variation as wide as from $127.26 to $14.08 between states—a ratio of 9 to 1. Strangely enough, this study of states, made by one who had access to the same type of records as those used by Commissioner Harris, brings out the same general conclusion made almost twenty years earlier. The wealthier states are still expending the most money per unit each year. Norton says in his study:

The states with the larger number of units of economic power per unit of educational need provide the larger amounts of educational support per child of school age, pay their teachers the higher salaries, pro-

[15] Russell, William F., Holy, Thos. C., Stone, Raleigh W. and Others of the Iowa Staff, *The Financing of Education in Iowa*, Vol. 8, p. 48, 1925.

[16] Sears, Jesse B. and Cubberley, Ellwood P., *The Cost of Education in California*, pp. 135-48, 1924.

[17] *Ibid.*

vide greater support per pupil in average daily attendance of non-salary costs, and maintain more substantial school plants per pupil enrolled.[18]

Another tentative conclusion which Dr. Norton discusses is that, while the states tend to expend different amounts per pupil, they tend to put forth a similar amount of effort. Since this does not hold true for counties in Florida and since the richer counties tend to expend greater amounts per unit, it seems that the correction lies not in uniformity of school practices and policies but in arranging for a degree of uniformity of ability after which will come either a higher degree of uniformity of practice and policies, or development in different directions, or both.

The historical background of this problem, as developed in the foregoing paragraphs, discloses considerable agreement in findings for different sections of the country. The degree of variation differs slightly from place to place. The relationships indicated differ considerably Yet, there is no reason to suppose that the several writers are not in agreement. The apparent discrepancy is probably a result of attacking the problem from different angles.

The determination of the degree of variation existing among school units should, in itself, be of value to those responsible for educational policies within a state. If the situation warrants correction, a beginning can be made from this point. When certain outstanding causes are known, modification of practice for purposes of correction may be effected, if such modification is desirable.

METHODS USED

From the sources used and the type of problem presented, it follows that the methods used should be analytical, statistical, and logical.

The procedure consists of five steps:

Step 1. Analysis of current expenditures of Florida counties by functions to determine the degree of variation which exists.

Step 2. Tabulation of those expenditures to show variation best.

Step 3. Analysis of probable relationships.

[18] Norton, J. K., "Ability of States to Support Education." *Research Bulletin of the National Education Associaton*, Vol. IV, No. 1, pp. 38 and 40.

Step 4. Tabulation of conditions relating variations.

Step 5. Correlation of measures of expenditures with measures of conditions for evidence of further relationships.

SOURCES OF DATA

The data for this problem were obtained chiefly from six sources:

1. Unpublished report of the Superintendent of Public Instruction, Florida, 1926-27.
2. County superintendent's reports, Florida counties, 1926-27.
3. United States Census Report.
4. Florida State Census Report.
5. Reports, Bureau of Internal Revenue.
6. Reports, United States Department of Agriculture.

LIMITATIONS OF THE STUDY

The manner in which the accounting systems of the schools of Florida are kept makes it impossible to separate distribution of expenditures for high school and elementary school. The salary ratio,[19] as used in the Educational Finance Inquiry, was attempted for this purpose, but the results were not usable. Hence, the idea of studying the expenditures separately was abandoned. It is recognized that this is a serious handicap, but, if the economic and sociological conditions under which a board works determine its educational policies, the effect will be felt in the high school and the elementary schools in much the same way, in so far as county comparisons are affected. Thus external conditions will affect the policies of a board of education relative to the high school in much the same way that they do with respect to the elementary schools.

It is clearly recognized that there are many factors affecting school expenditures which are not included in this study. For example, the personnel of the board of education or the school staff, the methods of supply purchase and supply management, or the political influences are all factors which will affect the per-pupil expenditures of a school system. Each of these is a comprehensive study in and of itself. School records in Florida are in such form that a study of these factors is rendered impossible.

[19] Strayer, George D. and Haig, Robert M., *The Financing of Education in the State of New York*, p. 43.

GENERAL OUTLINE

Three chapters will follow this introduction. Chapter II will deal with variation among counties in Florida. The variation of total current expense will be discussed. Then, to show variation within this total, each item will be analyzed.

Chapter III will deal with external conditions and internal factors related to this variation.

Chapter IV will be a summary of the preceding chapters.

The inclusion of both Negro and white schools has complicated the presentation of this problem. To eliminate one race or to discuss them separately seemed inadvisable. Since the degree of variation is so much greater among Negro schools than among white, their problems are considered by themselves in Chapter II. But conditions related to variation for the two races are in many cases similar if not identical. Therefore, the relationships and conclusions for both are given under the same subdivisions of Chapter III.

CHAPTER II

VARIATION IN SCHOOL EXPENDITURES

It is rather commonly thought by the people of the United States that this is a country of equal opportunity. We point to our schools with pride, and remark that the best thing in all our democracy is the fact that it does not matter where a person begins, for he may reach any height if he has the intelligence and ambition. We have put the schools to the service of every child in such a way that each has equal chance to progress. In this connection, Herbert Hoover [1] says:

> What do people mean by Democracy? Surely if they are speaking with any scientific exactness, they must mean only one thing. Democracy is a philosophy, or a system, under which for all men and women, to the utmost degree feasible, there is an absolute equality of opportunity, economic, political, and educational. That is what Democracy is now.

And after speaking of the origin of our creative leadership, he continues:

> Our leadership rises as if in capillary tubes, from that great underground river of increasing human capacity and integrity, latent and recessive in one generation of a family, let us say, but breaking out triumphant in the next.

He then goes on to say that it is our schools which give us equality of opportunity.

Such opinion seems to be quite general, yet if per-pupil expenditure is a measure of this opportunity, examination of the facts discloses gross inequalities. It would be difficult to conceive of one district purchasing for one dollar the same quality of educational service for which another must pay eight dollars. It is even difficult to imagine that equivalent educational service can be purchased in one county for half of what it costs in another. Yet, in Florida, the variation existing indicates that either there is no equality of educational opportunity or it is purchased at widely differing costs.

[1] Ward, William, "Education," *Good Housekeeping*, June, 1928, p. 248.

The amount which a county spends currently for education is the best measure of what that county is doing for its children. Any money which is spent intermittently may misrepresent the actual condition for any county in a given year. For this reason, the amount spent per pupil in average daily attendance for current expense is used as a measure for comparison.

Variation in Expenditures Among Schools for White Pupils
CURRENT EXPENSE

Current expense per pupil varies widely among Florida counties. The high paying county pays eight times as much for this purpose as does the low paying county. The median county pays only one-third as much as the high county. It pays three times as much as the low county. Table 1 shows these variations. Examination of this table shows variation between the county of the third quartile and the county of the first quartile of 2 to 1.

TABLE 1

Summary of Per-Pupil Expenditures for Elementary and High Schools Combined, for Whites, By Function Florida Counties, 1926–1927

Based on unpublished figures from the Office of the State Superintendent of Public Instruction

	General Control	Instructional Service	Auxiliary Agencies	Operation of Plant	Maintenance of Plant	Fixed Charges	Total Current Expense	Debt Service	Capital Outlay
High	$97.65	$130.61	$35.70	$7.75	$31.48	$4.64	$199.77	$146.17	$282.72
Q₃	17.41	57.44	9.31	3.03	5.23	1.51	91.67	43.62	60.67
Median	10.27	41.61	4.40	1.76	2.50	0.94	69.72	28.74	23.40
Q₁	4.97	34.32	2.81	0.69	1.01	0.54	51.16	17.34	4.04
Low	1.59	17.86	0.50	0.16	0.19	0.10	24.40	0.00	0.38

If the functions of the distribution which make up current expense are examined, even wider variation is found.

INSTRUCTIONAL SERVICE

The amount spent for instructional service, which is one of the best measures of what is actually done in the schoolroom, ranges from $17.86 to $130.61. If the amount expended for instructional service were the exact measure of what takes place in the schoolroom, the children of one county would be receiving education seven times as great as that received by children in another county. If it were assumed that the education of children in the counties represented in the middle fifty per cent of the cases were about equal, one county of this group expends nearly twice as much as another. The highest paying county expends three times as much as the median and the median two and one-half times as much as the lowest paying county.

When total current expense is divided into instructional service and other than instructional service, the variation is much greater for the latter than for instructional service. One county expends \$126.50 per pupil for total current expense while another expends only \$4.28—a ratio of 29 to 1; whereas for instructional service the ratio is only 7 to 1. The other ratios are correspondingly higher for other than instructional service. Since this is the smaller part of current expenditures, the extreme wide range is not reflected so much in total current expense where the ratio is as 8 to 1.

It is obvious from Table 2 that counties do not place equal stress on the instructional functions in their schools. Columns 4 and 5 show the percentage of total current expense used for in-

TABLE 2

Instructional Cost and Other Than Instructional Cost for Whites in Florida Counties, Summarized. Per Cent of Total Current Expense for Each, 1926–1927

Based on unpublished figures from the Office of the State Superintendent of Public Instruction

	Cost of Instructional Service per Pupil in A. D. A.	Cost of Other than Instructional Service	Percentage of Total for Current Expenses	Percentage of Other than Total of Current Expense
High	\$130.61	\$126.50	90.6%	84%
Q₃	57.44	34.67	74.0	43.6
Median ..	41.61	23.54	64.1	34.7
Q₁	34.32	12.57	56.3	25.9
Low	17.86	4.28	16.0	9.4

structional and other than instructional purposes, respectively. One county expends 90.6 per cent of total current expense for instructional service. Another expends almost as great a percentage for other than instructional purposes. On the other hand, one county expends as little as 16 per cent for instructional purposes. Another expends only 9.4 per cent for other purposes. The median cases represent just about average practice for the country. It should be observed in reading Table 2 that the per cents given in column 4 do not represent the same county as those in column 5.

GENERAL CONTROL

The amount spent in one county for general control for each pupil is $97.65, while the amount in the county expending the least per pupil for this function is only $1.59. The ratio here is as 61 to 1. The interquartile range is from $4.97 to $97.65. The high county pays nine times as much as the median county and the median county pays six times as much as the low county, for this function. This would indicate that one county is provided with very much better school leadership than another or that there is much waste in the high county.

AUXILIARY AGENCIES

In Florida, the major portion of the money distributed to auxiliary agencies is expended for transportation of pupils. For this reason, it might be expected that wide variation would be found. Transportation is not as necessary in one county as in another. The degree of variation here is 74 to 1.

OPERATION AND MAINTENANCE

It might be expected that the amount spent for operation and maintenance would show considerable variation since Florida counties are represented by those which have to heat buildings and those which do not. But it would hardly be expected that the range would be as wide as 195 to 1. One county expends $39.23 for these functions combined, while another expends only $.19. The high county spends nine times as much as the median and the median county twenty times as much as the low county. The interquartile range is represented by a ratio of 781 to 195, or about 4 to 1.

FIXED CHARGES

The amount expended for fixed charges suggests just as wide differences in practice as is represented by the other functions of the distribution. The respective degrees of variance for high over low, high over median, median over low, and interquartile range are represented by the figures 46 to 1.5, 1.9 to 1, and 9 to 1.

DEBT SERVICE

The debt service among counties in Florida varies from $146.17 to no debt service at all. There are two counties among the latter class. Of the counties which do expend money for debt service, the county which stands highest uses eight times as much money as the lowest. Even this range—from high to Q_1—is wide. The high paying county expends five times as much for debt service as the median county.

CAPITAL OUTLAY

It is not our purpose to study causes of variation for expenditures which are not a part of the current program, but it is of interest to note that the variation for capital outlay is even wider than that for current expense. The high county for buildings and equipment spends 744 times as much as the low county. The interquartile range is from $60.67 to $4.04 instead of $56.67, nearly two and one-half times as great as the amount spent by the median county.

Variation in Expenditures Among Schools for Negro Pupils

CURRENT EXPENSE

Current expense shows wider variation among schools for Negroes than among schools for white children. It is much wider than the variation shown in the other studies. The ratio of high to low is as 44 to 1. It is noticeable here, as in each of the functions making up current expense, that there is a sharp dropping off in the amount paid by the one hundredth percentile case and that of the seventy-fifth percentile case. The latter is only a little more than ten times as great as that represented by the lowest case. The median case is five times as great as the lowest case and the ratio of the twenty-fifth percentile is as great as 2½ to 1.

Inspection of Table 3 which represents per-pupil expenditures for Negro schools discloses even greater variation in every function than is found among counties for white children.

TABLE 3

SUMMARY OF PER-PUPIL EXPENDITURES FOR ELEMENTARY AND HIGH SCHOOLS COMBINED, FOR NEGROES, BY FUNCTION FLORIDA COUNTIES, 1926–1927

Based on unpublished figures from the Office of the State Superintendent of Public Instruction

	GEN-ERAL CON-TROL	IN-STRUC-TIONAL SERV-ICE	AUX-ILIARY AGEN-CIES	OPER-ATION OF PLANT	MAIN-TE-NANCE OF PLANT	FIXED CHARGES	TOTAL CUR-RENT EX-PENSE	DEBT SERV-ICE	CAPI-TAL OUT-LAY
High	$42.83	$35.62	(*)	$2.41	$11.99*	$3.15	$93.00	$56.23	$79.63
Q₃	2.44	17.96		.735	1.80	.49	21.60	7.71	20.94
Median	1.40	9.92		.28	.33	.15	11.33	3.48	1.66
Q₁	.49	5.19		.092	.13	.06	5.70	2.00	.32
Low	.07	1.71		.01	.03	.01	2.10	.30	.01

* Not enough cases reported for consideration.

INSTRUCTIONAL SERVICE

The degree of variation is not as wide for instructional service. The county paying the most for instructional service spends only twenty-one times as much as the county paying the least for this function. The seventy-fifth percentile county pays nearly eleven times as much as the low county. Here again, the difference between the median and low county is great—the median is nearly six times as great as the low. Even the twenty-fifth percentile amount is three times as great as the low. The range of the middle fifty per cent is from $17.96 to $5.19, about 3 to 1. This is more than the median amount paid, by about 22 per cent.

When total current expense is divided into instructional and noninstructional service, the variation in the latter is much greater than that which was found for whites. If one county is eliminated, however, the variation is not so great. This corresponds with the situation found in all other functions for Negroes. In the case of the Negroes, noninstructional service variation markedly affects the variation for total current expenses. This is rather surprising, since it is quite usual for schools paying little for teachers' salaries to expend small amounts also for other than instructional service. The schools for Negroes disclose a larger percentage of total current expense paid for instructional service than is the case for white schools. This is to be expected, however, since there is also a greater percentage of Negro schools of the one-teacher type. In one-teacher schools, the salary is usually the major part of total current expense. There is one county, however, which expends as much as 81.1 per cent for other than instructional purposes.

TABLE 4

INSTRUCTIONAL COST AND OTHER THAN INSTRUCTIONAL COST FOR NEGROES IN FLORIDA COUNTIES, SUMMARIZED. PER CENT OF TOTAL CURRENT EXPENSE FOR EACH, 1926–1927

Based on unpublished figures from the Office of the State Superintendent of Public Instruction

	COST OF INSTRUCTIONAL SERVICE PER PUPIL IN A. D. A.	COST OF OTHER THAN INSTRUCTIONAL SERVICE	PERCENTAGE OF TOTAL FOR CURRENT EXPENSES	PERCENTAGE OF OTHER THAN TOTAL OF CURRENT EXPENSES
High	$35.62	$57.83	96%	81.1%
Q₃	17.96	3.83	90.8	24.1
Median ..	19.92	1.68	84.4	15.0
Q₁	5.19	.77	76.4	9.2
Low	1.71	.20	28.9	3.47

GENERAL CONTROL

Some counties spend almost nothing for general control for Negroes. On the other hand, some spend more for this function alone than is spent for total current expense in others. The high county spends 612 times as much as the lowest. Comparing the third quartile with the low county, we find that it is thirty-four times as great. The median county spends twenty times as much. Even the twenty-fifth percentile county spends seven times as much as the lowest.

It is recognized that there is a fallacy in the method of obtaining the amount for this function, since it is easily conceivable that counties furnishing adequate funds for other functions for Negroes may not place any stress on the supervision for them. The figure for general control is based on the percentage of money expended for Negro schools for other purposes than general control.

AUXILIARY AGENCIES

There were only four counties in Florida which reported any expenditure for schools for Negroes which could be distributed to auxiliary agencies. Even here wide variation is shown, but because of the small number of cases it is not considered further.

OPERATION AND MAINTENANCE

It would seem that the upkeep and cleanliness of school buildings for Negroes is a very minor consideration in some Florida counties. One county spends only three cents per pupil for operation and maintenance. On the other hand, one county spends $12.40, or 413 times as much as the first-mentioned county. The seventy-fifth percentile, the median, and the twenty-fifth percentile are seventy-eight, twenty-two, and six times, respectively, as great as the lowest amount.

FIXED CHARGES

The amounts paid for fixed charges are as small as those paid for operation and maintenance. Only one cent per pupil is paid for this function by one county. Another county pays as much as $3.15. The third quartile county pays forty-nine times as much as the low county; the median fifteen times as much; and the first quartile county six times as much.

DEBT SERVICE

It was assumed that the schools for Negroes would spend for debt service as great a proportion of the total expenditures as the capital outlay plus the other expenditure is of the total expenditure. This seems a fair assumption. The high paying county expends 188 times as much as the low paying county. Again, the dropping off between the one hundredth and the seventy-fifth percentile is noticeable. The seventy-fifth percentile case is twenty-six, the median case is nearly twelve, and the twenty-fifth percentile case is nearly seven times as great as the first percentile case.

CAPITAL OUTLAY

Variation in capital outlay expenditure offers no exception to the rule for Negro schools. In fact, of the counties which spent anything, only one cent per pupil was spent for this purpose in 1926-27. This is one cent better than quite a number of counties paid. By comparing the amounts for each case represented in Table 4, the ratio is readily seen.

That counties of Florida do not exhibit as uniform practice for expenditure as is shown by other units studied in other states is evident from the variations shown above. While the variability is greater, the conditions affecting variation are likely not dissimilar. Examination for conditions affecting variation will be made in the following chapter.

CHAPTER III

CONDITIONS RELATED TO VARIATION

The interaction of many educational, sociological, and economical forces is related closely to variation in school expenditures. Conditions are here discussed under two general classifications; namely, those educational policies which a board initiates and those conditions over which a board has no control. The educational policies of a board of education, as determined from the objective evidence shown by their current expenditures, will be considered first. Then, the conditions over which a board of education exercises no control, but which of necessity influence them in their policies, will be investigated.

FACTORS WITHIN THE SCHOOL SYSTEM WHICH ARE RELATED TO THE AMOUNT OF EXPENDITURES

LENGTH OF TERM

White Schools. It will be seen from Table 5 that the schools in counties with longer terms on the average tend to spend more money per pupil in average daily attendance than do the schools in counties having shorter terms. While this is the general trend, specific cases show variation from this tendency. The county in Florida spending the most money has a session of from 150 to 160 days only. This is the exception. On the other hand, counties with the longer session—170 to 180 days—tend to spend more per pupil. Those with the shorter term—140 to 150 days— spend less.

The high expenditure of noninstructional service is the factor which makes the total current expense of the exceptional group higher than that of the other groups.

The third column of Table 5 shows that instructional service expenditures are highest for the term of 160 to 170 days.

The conclusion that this is the length of term for which full yearly salaries are paid seems probable. On the other hand,

21

TABLE 5

COMPARISON OF INSTRUCTIONAL COST AND OTHER THAN INSTRUCTIONAL
COST FOR WHITES IN FLORIDA COUNTIES CLASSIFIED ACCORD-
ING TO LENGTH OF TERM—FLORIDA, 1926–1927

*Based on unpublished figures from the Office of the State Superintendent of
Public Instruction*

LENGTH OF TERM IN DAYS	TOTAL CURRENT EXPENSE PER PUPIL	COST OF INSTRUCTIONAL SERVICE PER PUPIL	COST OF OTHER THAN INSTRUCTIONAL SERVICE PER PUPIL	NUMBER OF CASES (66)
170 to 180	Highest $ 94.23 Median 80.82 Lowest 69.55	Highest $ 60.38 Median 50.28 Lowest 36.19	Highest $33.85 Median 30.54 Lowest 24.07	4
160 to 170	Highest $150.55 Median 89.86 Lowest 41.46	Highest $ 90.31 Median 52.86 Lowest 26.57	Highest $56.77 Median 37.00 Lowest 7.44	26
150 to 160	Highest $158.22 Median 78.63 Lowest 49.16	Highest $ 65.88 Median 47.98 Lowest 34.69	Highest $87.29 Median 30.65 Lowest 11.11	10
140 to 150	Highest $144.13 Median 66.18 Lowest 33.45	Highest $130.61 Median 45.01 Lowest 22.30	Highest $56.34 Median 21.17 Lowest 9.60	15
130 to 140	Highest $ 47.71 Median 36.71 Lowest 26.96	Highest $ 35.14 Median 28.72 Lowest 21.95	Highest $12.57 Median 7.99 Lowest 4.56	4
120 to 130	Highest $103.44 Median 47.81 Lowest 26.38	Highest $ 25.25 Median 21.64 Lowest 20.12	Highest $ 8.89 Median 6.42 Lowest 4.28	4
96 to 120	Highest $ 51.94 Median 36.03 Lowest 25.13	Highest $ 34.99 Median 25.12 Lowest 17.86	Highest $16.95 Median 10.91 Lowest 7.27	3

the term of 150 to 160 days represents those counties expending the greatest amount for other than instructional service.
It is probable that schools having longer terms are in a position
to purchase and manage other services more advantageously and
more uniformly. Those having shorter terms probably furnish
less of this kind of service. It is evident from these facts that
while differing lengths of terms are related to variation, only a
certain percentage of the variation follows this relationship.

Negro Schools. As will be seen in Table 6, the same tendency
for counties with longer terms to cost more per pupil than those
with shorter terms is found among schools for Negroes. Those

TABLE 6

COMPARISON OF INSTRUCTIONAL COST AND OTHER THAN INSTRUCTIONAL
COST FOR NEGROES IN FLORIDA COUNTIES CLASSIFIED
ACCORDING TO LENGTH OF TERM—FLORIDA, 1926-1927

*Based on unpublished figures from the Office of the State Superintendent of
Public Instruction*

LENGTH OF TERM IN DAYS	TOTAL CURRENT EXPENSE PER PUPIL		COST OF INSTRUCTIONAL SERVICE PER PUPIL		COST OF OTHER THAN INSTRUCTIONAL SERVICE PER PUPIL		NUMBER OF CASES (65)
160 to 180	Highest $	43.72	Highest $	30.62	Highest	$13.10	4
	Median	31.05	Median	23.03	Median	8.02	
	Lowest	23.21	Lowest	16.28	Lowest	1.69	
150 to 160	Highest $	93.00	Highest $	35.62	Highest	$57.38	8
	Median	33.64	Median	21.07	Median	12.56	
	Lowest	16.73	Lowest	14.30	Lowest	1.28	
140 to 150	Highest $	51.80	Highest $	17.80	Highest	$36.83	2
	Median	37.39	Median	16.39	Median	21.01	
	Lowest	22.98	Lowest	14.97	Lowest	5.18	
130 to 140	Highest $	32.19	Highest $	30.90	Highest	$10.74	7
	Median	25.01	Median	20.31	Median	4.69	
	Lowest	20.21	Lowest	15.97	Lowest	1.29	
120 to 130	Highest $	23.52	Highest $	19.85	Highest	$ 4.98	4
	Median	18.11	Median	14.43	Median	3.68	
	Lowest	15.11	Lowest	10.13	Lowest	2.80	
100 to 120	Highest $	38.56	Highest $	15.75	Highest	$22.81	6
	Median	16.31	Median	11.26	Median	5.05	
	Lowest	9.47	Lowest	8.33	Lowest	1.04	
90 to 100	Highest $	9.98	Highest $	9.04	Highest	$ 2.70	6
	Median	8.34	Median	7.22	Median	1.11	
	Lowest	5.70	Lowest	5.09	Lowest	.40	
80 to 90	Highest $	15.83	Highest $	14.64	Highest	$ 3.22	11
	Median	9.58	Median	7.98	Median	1.60	
	Lowest	3.69	Lowest	3.34	Lowest	.35	
70 to 80	Highest $	7.17	Highest $	5.78	Highest	$ 1.39	6
	Median	4.67	Median	3.97	Median	.70	
	Lowest	3.35	Lowest	3.03	Lowest	.26	
60 to 70	Highest $	8.86	Highest $	6.92	Highest	$ 1.94	7
	Median	4.32	Median	3.72	Median	.60	
	Lowest	2.43	Lowest	2.16	Lowest	.20	
30 to 50	Highest $	22.43	Highest $	20.76	Highest	$ 1.67	4
	Median	8.37	Median	7.57	Median	.80	
	Lowest	2.10	Lowest	1.71	Lowest	.39	

costing most have terms of 150 to 160 days. There is an exception to this tendency in the group having terms of 100 to 120 days. One reason for this is suggested in Table 6, where it will be seen that the high county spends a large amount for other than instructional service. Of this amount, nearly one half is expended for auxiliary agencies and more than half for general control.

The group having a term of 30 to 50 days is also exceptional. The high county here spends 80 per cent of its current expense fund for teachers' salaries. Overemphasis on any item of the budget tends to raise expenditures in spite of the length of term.

A large amount of the money which a county pays for education is spent for teachers' salaries. The amount of salary paid is a condition over which a board of education exercises control. For these reasons, the length of term and the teacher's salary were correlated. The coefficient is .705 ± .06. If size of school is held constant, the residual correlation between length of term and teachers' salaries is .65. The correlation between salary and a combination of length of term and size of school is .715.

Correlations were calculated for these variables in connection with schools for Negroes. The correlation between length of term and teachers' salary in these schools is .85 ± .01. When the total relation between salary and a combination of length of term and size of school is calculated, the correlation is .878. If the factor, size of school, is held constant, the residual correlation is .659.

The correlation between length of term and cost per pupil was computed for both white schools and Negro schools. The correlation was .63 ± .06 for white and .69 ± .09 for Negro schools. There is a greater tendency for current expense cost for Negroes to rise with increasing length of term than there is for whites.

Longer terms are more economical because they reach more pupils. The larger schools have longer terms, as indicated by the fact that there is a correlation of .775 ± .04 between number of pupils per school and the length of term for white schools, and .616 ± .05, for Negro schools. Both instructional and other than instructional service may be purchased more efficiently for these schools because there are more pupils.

Summary. Since the length of term increases as the salary cost for teacher and the current expense cost per pupil increase, the relationships indicate controls which are set up to govern cost. Tables 5 and 6 and the correlation coefficients quoted above show similar trends. The tables show some exceptions while the coefficients of correlation give proper weight to each case and thus show the average relationship.

SIZE OF SCHOOL

As was stated in Chapter I, it was impossible to separate current expense for elementary schools from current expense for high schools. The best that could be done, then, was to compare elementary schools on the basis of teachers' salaries. Schools were classified according to the number of teachers in each.

White Schools. From the summary of the schools for whites given in Table 7, it is clear that the annual cost per pupil for one-teacher schools is practically the same as that found in schools having from twenty to twenty-nine teachers. It is apparent that the low cost incident to having more pupils in larger schools is offset by added educational opportunity. Those medium-sized schools in Florida counties ranging from two to nineteen teachers are more economical per pupil to operate than one-teacher schools, in spite of the fact that they offer more opportunity. Medium-sized schools, with from two to nineteen teachers, are also less expensive per pupil than larger schools.

The greatest amount of variation is found in one-teacher schools. This corresponds with the degree of variation in the number of pupils in them. Teachers' salaries vary also. And since there is very little relationship between the number of pupils per teacher and the teacher's salary, the wide variation in cost per pupil results. Or, stated differently, in schools of more than one teacher there is a tendency to equalize the number of pupils per teacher.

Schools with three to four teachers make impossible the assignment of pupils to classes of uniform size. This accounts for the variability in school expenditures for this group.

The schools having five to nine teachers show least variability of any schools of the smaller type. On the whole, these schools cost less per pupil than any other type. It seems that this is the point at which the curriculum is limited to the minimum essentials and the number of pupils per teacher is not so varied.

The large schools show very little variability. It may be assumed that these schools are standardized as to procedure, salary, and number of pupils per teacher.

Elementary white teachers in Florida counties may expect to receive higher salaries if they are placed in larger schools. In schools having the greater number of teachers, the demands for professional qualifications are greater and salaries are correspondingly higher. The correlation coefficient between size of school, as determined by number of teachers, and teacher's salary is .319 ± .07 for white schools. It is much higher for Negro schools (.659 ± .05). These facts conform in general with conditions found in other parts of the United States.

Negro Schools. The school which costs only $1.60 per pupil

TABLE 7

EXPENDITURES PER PUPIL IN AVERAGE DAILY ATTENDANCE FOR TEACHERS' SALARIES, ELEMENTARY SCHOOLS FOR WHITES, SUMMARIZED—FLORIDA, 1926-1927

Based on unpublished figures from the Office of State Superintendent of Public Instruction

	NUMBER OF TEACHERS							
	1	2	3–4	5–9	10–19	20–29	30–49	50–75
Highest ..	$163.64	$107.14	$169.43	$82.69	$93.50	$65.04	$53.67	$43.98
Q_1	59.51	51.73	49.20	48.40	44.45	53.64	......	.....
Median ..	43.35	34.57	35.49	36.47	35.06	41.68	49.20	40.82
Q_3	24.96	21.60	26.80	29.92	28.84	34.70	......	.....
Lowest ..	11.82	11.34	13.26	15.21	11.85	9.52	38.63	39.46

for teacher's salary is scarcely conceivable. Yet this describes a one-teacher Negro school in a county of Florida. This is shown in Table 8. These schools vary for teacher's salary from $55.33 to $1.60 per pupil in average daily attendance. In the median county the cost per pupil is $8.22. The county which costs only $1.60 per pupil for teacher's salary is a school where a teacher has many pupils and yet receives a low salary. The opposite condition may be expected in the county expending $55.83 per pupil for the same service.

Two-teacher Negro schools show less variability. The tendency seems to be toward small salaries with the number of children per teacher still high. When the number of teachers in the school is increased from five to nine, added opportunities seem to offset the effect of fewer students. The larger Negro schools tend to be more economical; they are large enough to be standardized and to assign students more advantageously.

The correlation between size of school and length of term, as determined by the number of teachers, is .406 ± .07 for white schools and .574 ± .05 for Negro schools. The larger schools have longer terms. When size of school is determined by the average number of pupils and correlated with length of term, the coefficients are .755 ± .05 and .612 ± .06 for white and Negro counties, respectively. Since counties with larger schools are those having centers of population, it is to be expected that school will be in session longer.

The correlation between size of school (number of teachers) and teacher's salary is .319 ± .08 and .659 ± .07 for white and

TABLE 8

EXPENDITURES PER PUPIL IN AVERAGE DAILY ATTENDANCE FOR TEACHERS' SALARIES, ELEMENTARY SCHOOLS FOR NEGROES, SUMMARIZED—FLORIDA, 1926–1927

Based on unpublished figures from the Office of State Superintendent of Public Instruction

	NUMBER OF TEACHERS					
	1	2	3–4	5–9	10–19	20–29
Highest	$55.33	$26.83	$28.26	$89.46	$63.22	$26.83
Q_1	12.81	14.86	18.93	24.95	....	....
Median	8.22	7.18	9.28	16.92	18.52	17.30
Q_3	4.63	4.49	5.33	12.45	....	....
Lowest	1.60	1.56	1.51	5.65	5.34	10.99
Number of Cases	60	43	36	21	15	6

Negro schools, respectively. The correlation of a combination of length of term and size of school with salary is .715 and .878, respectively, for white and Negro schools. When length of term is held constant for Negro and white schools, the residual *r*'s are .16 and .397, respectively.

In every case, it seems that teachers' salaries for Negro schools are more dependent upon size of school than upon teachers' salaries for white schools.

Size of Class

In Table 9, the counties of Florida are classified according to the average size of classes. It will be seen from this that the larger classes tend to be in the larger schools. By comparing column 4 with column 2, a corresponding observation can be made. The classes are larger as the percentage of one-teacher schools in the total number of schools decreases. It can be concluded from

TABLE 9

Comparison of Average Size of Class with Average Number of Pupils Per School. Average Teacher's Salary and Per Cent of One-Teacher Schools—Negro and White

Florida Counties, 1926–27

Counties Ranked by Size of Class	Average Size of Class	Average Number Pupils per School	Per Cent of One-Teacher Schools
White:			
First Group	23.4–41.7	169.	34.4
Second Group	21.1–33.3	97.9	36.4
Third Group	18.2–21.1	75.7	47.6
Fourth Group	9.1–18.1	82.4	51.0
Negro:			
First Group	34.5–54.1	88.6	70.0
Second Group	30.1–34.3	75.	73.0
Third Group	26.9–30.0	86.	64.0
Fourth Group	13.5–26.7	47.6	57.0

these facts that the variation in per-pupil cost in one-teacher schools is due chiefly to variation in the number of pupils; that is, the effect of the varying number of pupils in small classes is more noticeable than similar variations would be in large classes. Since it is possible in the large schools to equalize the teaching load, variation because of variability in number of pupils per teacher is not so great.

Degree of Consolidation

Consolidated school systems tend to bring larger numbers of pupils together. As a rule, more transportation is furnished or less is needed. Hence, the cost per pupil for education may be expected to vary according to the degree to which a county is consolidated.

If the per cent of white pupils transported in each county can be taken as a measure of consolidation and if this measure is correlated with current expense per pupil for whites, it seems not to affect the amount spent. The correlation is .05 ± .07. The explanation lies in the fact that in the counties where transportation is necessary, the amount of wealth available prohibits large amounts of expenditures for any purpose whatsoever. On the other hand, wealthy or densely populated counties do not need transportation and hence are not included in this measure of consolidation.

Indebtedness and Debt Service

It would ordinarily be expected that counties which had involved themselves in heavy indebtedness for school purposes would effect economies in current expenditures to mitigate the burden on the taxpayers. Apparently, Florida counties have not reached the point where they find indebtedness burdensome enough to warrant restraint of the current educational program in order that the debts may be paid without unduly burdening the taxpayers. In fact, the indebtedness seems to have no relation to the amount spent for current expenses.

When the per cent of indebtedness based on full valuation is calculated and this per cent is compared with expenditure per pupil in average daily attendance for current expense, there is in evidence a very slight tendency for those counties which are heavily indebted to correspond with those which spend larger amounts per unit for current expense. Stated differently, those counties which have little or no debt tend to spend less per unit for current expense.[1] The correlation is low (.002 ± .04). The variability in this respect, however, is so great as to vitiate any conclusion drawn.

When the taxable wealth of a county and the per cent of indebtedness are compared there is again a very slight tendency for

[1] Sears and Cubberley, *Cost of Education in California*, Vol. 7, pp. 227-228.

those counties having the most wealth to carry the lowest debt burden. This would indicate that poorer counties are attempting to keep pace even under burdensome taxes. While the correlation coefficient for taxable wealth and indebtedness is only — .17 ± .08, it is worthy of note because it is negative.

There seems to be no relation between the degree to which a county has obligated itself and the amount it spends for each pupil for current expenses. On the other hand, a county which expends a large amount for debt service tends to spend a large amount for current expenses per unit. The correlation between debt service and cost per pupil for current expense is .578 ± .05. This may be interpreted in two ways: (1) the counties which obligate themselves more are called upon to supply more service currently; and (2) the counties which give better current service are also willing to mortgage their wealth for permanent improvement.

Capital Outlay

Since the capital outlay figure for any county in any one year may not represent that county's policy for building, the average cost per pupil for the past three years was taken as a measure of a board's capital outlay policy. When this amount is compared with the amount spent per pupil for current expense, it is very evident that the counties which have spent the most on the average for capital outlay are the ones which spend greater amounts for current expense. Stated differently, expenditure for capital outlay does not induce economy for other purposes. The county which builds thereby raises its operation, maintenance, and instructional cost along with insurance and other items of current expense. This may be seen from Table 10.

Of the seventeen counties spending most for capital outlay, ten are among the first quarter when classified according to true wealth. Thirteen of the seventeen counties spending least for capital outlay are among the fifty per cent having the least amount of wealth. The counties which spend more for capital outlay also spend more for current expense. But they also tend to be the wealthier counties.

What has been said of capital outlay with respect to current expense may also be said concerning expenditure for debt service. The county which expends most for capital outlay also expends most for debt service. Since capital outlay is usually a result of sale of bonds, it follows that debt service for these bonds would correspond.

TABLE 10

RELATION OF CAPITAL OUTLAY, 1924–1925–1926–1927, TO CURRENT EXPENSE AND DEBT SERVICE, 1926–1927
NEGRO AND WHITE COMBINED

COUNTIES RANKED IN GROUPS	RANGE OF COST FOR CAPITAL OUTLAY PER PUPIL	CURRENT EXPENSE PER PUPIL	DEBT SERVICE PER PUPIL
First Group	$39.66–$106.18	$114.22	$55.20
Second Group	14.24– 37.23	89.09	47.62
Third Group	3.19– 12.37	78.20	29.70
Fourth Group	10– 3.09	70.59	20.33

CONDITIONS OUTSIDE OF THE SCHOOL SYSTEM WHICH ARE RELATED TO THE AMOUNT OF EXPENDITURES

It seems reasonable to assume that a board of education is influenced in its decisions by conditions over which it has no control. A 180-day session of school may be desired, but if shortage of funds makes this impossible, the board must of necessity decide upon a shorter term and thus curtail expenditures. This same condition may affect policies regarding teaching loads or any other policy within its control.

TYPE OF POPULATION

Does the type of population affect the amount spent currently for educational purposes? To answer this question three measures were calculated:

1. The per cent of Negroes in the total population.
2. The per cent of total population coming from southern states.
3. The per cent of population coming from other than southern states.

The fact that smaller schools tend to spend less for teachers' salaries suggests the idea that there may be a difference in the type of population patronizing these schools or in the amount of wealth with which this population purchases its educational

opportunities.   Harris [2] showed that southern states spent less
per unit for school purposes than other groups in a geographical
classification.   The suggestion follows that the presence of
Negroes in the population may influence the money spent per
unit for white schools.

The measures used in this study are based upon the 1925
Florida State Census.   That the accuracy of this census may be
questioned was understood and anticipated.   The chief of the
U.S. Census Bureau was asked in a personal letter for an opinion.   His expression of the situation follows:

> While we are not in a position to express an opinion as to the rela-
> tive accuracy of the different state censuses, the fact that we are using
> the Florida census as a basis for our annual estimates indicates that we
> have found it satisfactory for this purpose.   I believe that the principal
> reason for criticism of the available population figures for Florida is mainly
> the result of the fact that the census was taken just before the boom of
> 1925 and 1926 and that great increase especially in the population of some
> of the cities, took place after the state census enumeration was com-
> pleted. . . .
> Even though the 1925 enumeration may be somewhat incomplete, the
> incompleteness will probably affect very little such ratios and percentages
> as those mentioned in your letter.

If this opinion is accepted, the measures which are used here
will be an understatement rather than an overstatement; and,
while conservative, they will be approximately correct.

It was therefore decided that in the percentages used for this
study the errors would not be so great as to affect the conclusions which might be deduced.

In order to determine the relation between the per cent of
Negroes in the total population and the cost per pupil for white
schools, the correlation was calculated and found to be .11 $\pm$ .08.
From this it seems safe to say that the counties of Florida provide education for white children according to the standards of
each county, regardless of the Negro population.

When the correlation between the per cent of Negro "pupila-
tion" in the total population and the cost per pupil for Negro
schools is calculated, the coefficient is 0.21 $\pm$ .08.   Again, the
correlation is too small to warrant definite conclusion.   It indicates, however, that there is a tendency for the counties which

[2] Harris, W. H.   "Conditions Which Cause Variation in the Rate of School Expenditure."   *Proceedings of Department of Superintendence*, pp. 53-54.

have a larger proportion of Negroes to spend less per pupil for their education.

It would seem from these facts that causes for low per-pupil expenditures for white children in counties of Florida do not lie in the proportion of Negro population.

Comparison of Florida counties on the basis of per cent of population coming from southern states indicates that this factor makes no significant difference. The correlation (.15 ± .08) is too slight to be significant. The influx of population, however, from northern, western, and mid-western states (grouped in this study as "northern") does seem to be related to increase in cost per pupil for current expenses. The correlation is .646 ± .049. Three reasons may be advanced for this relationship: (1) the people from northern states, accustomed to higher expenditures, tend to influence the expenditures in the counties where they locate; (2) the population from northern states brings wealth into the county; and (3) this population has located in wealthy counties. It is likely that the desire to pay taxes is no stronger among the population of one section than it is among that from another section. Hence the latter two reasons are no doubt the significant reasons for the relationships shown.

Correlation for these variables is very much the same for Negroes as it is for whites (.616 ± .054). The same reasons may be advanced as in (2) and (3) above.

The correlation of the wealth of a county with the per cent of population from southern states (.26 ± .085) supports the conclusion that the population from southern states is very much like the native population of the counties of Florida and therefore no effect of this incoming population is noticeable.

On the other hand, the high correlation between per cent of population from northern states and cost for current expense is matched by a similar high correlation when related to wealth (.532 ± .06). This correlation lends support to either of the theories: (1) this type of incoming population brings wealth with it or (2) it locates in counties where wealth exists.

The correlation between wealth and current expense for white population is .665 ± .05. The correlation between wealth and northern population is .532 ± .06. Where wealth is held constant the "northern" current expense residual is .46. This shows a relation between "northern" population and current expense

that is significant. The reason for this relationship can be sur-
mised. The incoming "northern" population brings wealth with
it and settles in counties with the existing wealth and, therefore,
spends more per pupil for education.

The wealth-current- expense-correlation residual when "northern" population is constant is .497. The combination of wealth
and "northern" population related with current expense cost
renders a coefficient of correlation of .749. With these relationships in mind, it can be reasoned that wealth plus incoming
heterogeneous population affects the policies of a board of education which, in turn, affect variation in school expenditures. This
population probably comes because of wealth inherent in the
county. The high paying counties for white population correspond closely with high paying counties for Negroes. It is therefore safe to assume that the same external factors affect the
policies for both.

WEALTH

The Crowell Publishing Company has ranked Florida counties for business purposes into four classes: (1) best counties,
(2) good counties, (3) fair counties, (4) poor counties.[3] This
ranking is based upon information derived from government
statistics.[4]

On this basis Table 11 shows that "best" counties spend
more for current expense than "poor" counties in a ratio of approximately three to two. While "good" and "fair" counties ap-
proximate each other in money spent for current expense, the
relationship between ratings and per-pupil current expense is
direct.

Column 3 of Table 11 compared with column 1 shows that
the relationship between county ratings and cost per pupil is
direct. The "best" counties spend nearly two and one-half times
as much as the "poor" counties; the "good" counties spend nearly
twice as much as the "poor"; and the "fair" counties spend 28
per cent more per pupil than the "poor."

[3] *The National Markets*, p. 45. Crowell Publishing Company.
[4] The United States Census of Population for 1920-22, the United States Census of
Manufacture for 1919, the United States Geological Survey for 1922-23, the Bureau of
Fisheries 1920-23, the United States Census of Agriculture for 1920, the United States
Bureau of Internal Revenue, 1923, R. L. Polk Co., Passenger Car Regulation, January 1,
1925. Number of Retail Outlets, 1922.

TABLE 11

BUSINESS RATINGS OF COUNTIES* COMPARED WITH CURRENT EXPENSES—
NEGRO AND WHITE
FLORIDA—1926–27

BUSINESS RATINGS	CURRENT EXPENSE PER PUPIL	
	White	Negro
Best	$97.94	$30.02
Good	76.70	22.26
Fair	80.70	15.68
Poor	64.11	12.22

* Rated by Crowell Publishing Company. *The National Markets*, p. 45.

Counties which have the greatest amount of real value [5] behind each pupil tend to expend the greatest amount per pupil for current expense, as will be seen from Table 14. The seventeen wealthiest counties spend nearly two and one-half times as much per pupil, on the average, as the sixteen counties having the least wealth. Even the two groups comprising the middle fifty per cent show a difference in their means of $15.86.

The second group spends 68 per cent more for current expense than the low group. The relationship is even more direct when Negro expenditures are considered. The first group spends about five times as much as the fourth group. The second and third groups, in turn, spend about four times and two times as much, respectively, as the fourth group.

Correlation between true wealth and current expense (.665 ± .05) supports the idea that wealthier counties tend to spend more current expense per pupil.

But true wealth is not a complete measure of a county's ability. It was therefore decided to use income as an index. Although the income in Florida cannot be taxed, it is an index of the ability to pay and it, therefore, does influence the amount of money spent. The most reliable income information available at this time is the estimate of the Crowell Publishing Company. It is not the purpose of this study to justify that estimate. It is being used by business enterprises as a basis for distribution policies and is the best available at the present time.

[5] Data from unpublished Survey of Schools of Florida.

TABLE 12

AVERAGE PER-PUPIL EXPENDITURES, TEACHERS' SALARIES ONLY, FOR WHITES FOR ELEMENTARY SCHOOLS CLASSIFIED ACCORDING TO NUMBER OF TEACHERS BY COUNTIES FLORIDA, 1926–1927

Based on unpublished figures from the Office of State Superintendent of Public Instruction

COUNTY	NUMBER OF TEACHERS								
	1	2	3–4	5–9	10–19	20–29	30–49	50–75	Over
Alachua ...	$ 28.39	$ 26.69	$ 28.24	$35.87	$34.79	......	......	$40.82	......
Baker	28.40	29.70	33.92	32.03	......				
Bay	35.11	27.05	35.34	37.20	29.88				
Bradford ...	25.23	22.11	39.95	36.65	28.79				
Brevard ...	49.45	58.62	83.45	......	93.50				
Broward ...	......	54.22	48.92	60.28	48.67	$54.43			
Calhoun ...	19.55	17.77	60.45	......	20.03				
Charlotte ..	85.17	66.67	......	81.37	39.27				
Citrus	56.32	65.07	44.01	49.50	......				
Clay	30.37	40.36	43.67	63.42	21.84	......			
Collier				(No Data)					
Columbia ..	22.83	16.59	50.11	34.76	42.76	......			
Dade	94.31	68.38	52.98	59.76	56.89	56.07	$45.43		
De Soto ...	43.27	35.33	31.64	31.24	33.46				
Dixie	43.43	......	62.73	......	48.69				
Duval	58.33	76.39	55.34	50.21	48.35	45.71			
Escambia ..	19.77	24.66	25.05	26.75	31.95				
Flagler	102.86	52.20	......	......	50.99				
Franklin ...	27.62	......							
Gadsen	26.40	34.69	13.43	30.92	31.21	39.01			
Gilchrist ...	19.99	21.08	......	28.04	38.69				
Glades	82.55	41.50	......	......	70.54				
Gulf	33.90	28.55	......						
Hamilton ..	16.20	20.68	14.98	39.14	30.47	......			
Hardee	29.06	25.29	31.93	19.92	17.72	9.52			
Hendry				(No Data)					
Hernando ..	47.36	36.80	41.69	27.16	......				
Highlands ..	61.61	36.71	60.72	82.69	......	53.38			
Hillsborough	53.23	33.91	25.36	28.69	33.85	35.75	38.63	43.98	......
Holmes	14.31	12.93	13.26	25.85	......	......	......	......	$147.61
Indian River	111.11	......	169.43	......					
Jackson ...	23.83	15.65	17.84	31.54	35.32	......			
Jefferson ...	30.00	31.67	38.56	44.12	......				
Lafayette ..	54.04	40.30	20.82	......	40.23				
Lake	44.90	51.26	49.49	47.94	35.88				
Lee	73.92	......	52.89	44.99	44.16				
Leon	47.36	......	39.06	39.40	......				
Levy	31.68	44.80	33.12	51.39	41.56				
Liberty	22.13	29.10	33.94	36.29	......				
Madison ...	24.58	26.41	18.08	32.13	34.41	41.68			
Manatee ...	38.73	41.88	21.24	26.09	36.80	37.34			
Marion	34.36	36.48	31.56	43.80	26.37	......			

TABLE 12 (*Continued*)

COUNTY	NUMBER OF TEACHERS								
	1	2	3–4	5–9	10–19	20–29	30–49	50–75	Over
Martin	$ 83.33	$ 72.51	$ 48.62	$73.07	....	....	....	....	....
Monroe	77.25	107.14	64.94	42.51	....	$34.93	....	....	....
Nassau	29.82	31.10	38.72	34.28	$43.09	....	....	....	....
Okaloosa ...	18.01	22.77	31.61	31.31	27.72	....	....	....	....
Okeechobee	60.69	70.65	....	....	31.77	....	....	....	....
Orange	61.08	49.29	35.64	53.89	28.99	....	$49.20	....	....
Osceola	37.69	....	71.77	60.45	....	65.04	53.67	....	....
Palm Beach	57.32	85.77	92.19	53.88	45.04	63.60	....	....	....
Pasco	50.31	38.12	29.22	37.67	24.82	....	....	....	....
Pinellas ...	....	55.84	40.17	33.48	44.55	43.56	....	....	....
Polk	29.84	27.51	35.27	35.42	26.52	26.71	....	....	$26.92
Putnam ...	163.64	31.97	50.20	38.19	....	36.53	....	....	....
St. Johns ..	61.94	52.50	....	22.39	40.54	33.48	....	....	....
St. Lucie ...				(No Data)					
Santa Rosa .	18.70	20.27	20.83	19.03	11.85	....	....	....	....
Sarasota ...	67.58	53.93	41.64	....	57.27	48.00	....	....	....
Seminole ...	40.81	16.26	43.01	....	....	....	....	$39.46	....
Sumter	36.06	34.48	43.59	40.56	32.07	....	....	....	....
Suwannee ..	11.82	16.81	30.16	15.21	....	....	....	....	....
Taylor	42.69	36.66	34.29	36.11	26.69	....	....	....	....
Union	22.14	11.34	16.10	20.46	33.95	....	....	....	....
Volusia	68.17	46.16	40.61	48.04	64.60	44.31	42.74	....	....
Wakulla ...	27.86	29.44	20.22	30.33	....	34.01	....	....	....
Washington	15.20	13.19	16.77	16.74	17.62	....	....	....	....
Highest	$163.64	$107.14	$169.43	$82.69	$93.50	$65.04	$53.67	$43.98	$147.61
Q₁	59.51	51.73	49.20	48.40	44.45	53.64	....	....	....
Median	43.35	34.57	35.49	36.47	35.06	41.68	49.20	40.82	....
Q₃	24.96	21.60	26.80	29.92	28.84	34.70	....	....	....
Lowest	11.82	11.34	13.26	15.21	11.85	9.52	38.63	39.46	26.92
Number of Cases ...	62	58	54	51	45	19	5	3	2

This income figure, plus one-tenth of the country's true wealth, was used as an index of wealth. Thus real value and income value are weighed for this figure. When it is correlated with the cost per pupil, the coefficient resulting is .646 ± .07, approximately the same as that between true wealth and cost per pupil for current expenses. It lends support to the conclusion that wealth is the factor causing variation.

It is of interest to note that while the wealthier counties spend more money for all types of school service, they can do so with the least effort, when effort is measured by the per cent of eco-

TABLE 13

AVERAGE PER-PUPIL EXPENDITURES, TEACHERS' SALARIES ONLY, FOR
NEGROES FOR ELEMENTARY SCHOOLS CLASSIFIED ACCORDING TO
NUMBER OF TEACHERS BY COUNTIES
FLORIDA, 1926–1927

Based on unpublished figures from the Office of State Superintendent of Public Instruction

COUNTY	NUMBER OF TEACHERS						
	1	2	3–4	5–9	10–19	20–29	30–49
Alachua	$ 5.31	$ 5.46	$ 7.70	$16.92	......	......	......
Baker	3.75	2.33	......	......	......	......	......
Bay	5.27	5.00	......	......	......	......	......
Bradford	2.30	2.18	9.04	......	......	......	......
Brevard	25.60	21.36	20.05	20.98	......	......	......
Broward	......	......	18.42	13.31	......	......	......
Calhoun				No Data			
Charlotte	42.00	......	29.58	......	......	......	......
Citrus	10.52	8.67	8.79	......	......	......	......
Clay	11.43	......	11.90	......	......	......	......
Collier				No Data			
Columbia	4.54	4.35	4.80	38.97	$12.09	......	......
Dade	21.70	22.19	34.18	32.11	63.22	$26.83	......
De Soto	7.09	......	......	......	15.74	......	......
Dixie	10.95	......	......	......	......	......	......
Duval	11.69	13.50	......	......	13.47	18.83	$27.11
Escambia	10.44	9.52	13.42	15.78	......	......	......
Flagler	21.18	......	......	......	......	......	......
Franklin	4.46	17.29	......	19.46	......	......	......
Gadsden	2.90	3.62	1.51	8.08	......	......	......
Gilchrist	1.60	......	......	......	......	......	......
Glades	3.98	......	......	......	......	......	......
Gulf	9.13	10.47	......	......	......	......	......
Hamilton	......	......	4.80	......	......	......	......
Hardee	4.38	3.70	3.75	......	......	......	......
Hendry				No Data			
Hernando	7.42	5.25	8.43	......	......	......	......
Highlands	15.72	......	8.67	......	......	......	......
Hillsborough	11.64	14.83	9.52	12.17	25.85	14.30	......
Holmes	6.77	7.28	......	......	......	......	......
Indian River	5.83	6.22	7.37	......	......	......	......
Jackson	5.72	3.54	5.33	......	......	......	......
Jefferson	2.53	1.56	4.24	......	......	......	......
Lafayette	14.49	......	......	......	......	......	......
Lake	10.45	14.93	16.19	25.82	......	......	......
Lee	44.33	......	......	......	21.57	......	......
Leon	3.63	......	......	......	12.67	......	......
Levy	6.07	4.91	5.22	......	......	......	......
Liberty	10.70	6.43	......	......	......	......	......
Madison	2.99	2.10	3.49	......	......	......	......
Manatee	5.33	4.54	6.75	11.44	22.38	......	......
Marion	5.72	5.40	......	......	......	......	......

TABLE 13 *(Continued)*

COUNTY	NUMBER OF TEACHERS						
	1	2	3–4	5–9	10–19	20–29	30–49
Martin	$55.33	26.38	....	27.88	....	....	....
Monroe	22.04	....	....	....	....	....	....
Nassau	11.14	....	$13.72	....	....	....	....
Okaloosa	6.57	$ 6.18	....	....	....	....	....
Okeechobee	....	14.63	....	....	....	....	....
Orange	20.20	16.99	14.63	14.49	....	....	$14.88
Osceola	18.70	12.82	12.75	21.51	....	....	....
Palm Beach	32.78	18.37	22.06	20.38	....	....	....
Pasco	14.98	17.29	....	10.47	....	....	....
Pinellas	12.81	18.68	23.29	....	$18.52	....	....
Polk	11.16	12.12	10.79	16.41	11.33	$15.80	....
Putnam	11.55	9.05	12.56	....	15.09	....	....
St. Johns	8.73	20.28	13.70	13.62	24.07	....	....
St. Lucie	....	....	....	....	....	24.62	....
Santa Rosa	3.44	3.85	....	....	....	....	....
Sarasota	25.26	....	....	....	21.95	....	....
Seminole	11.76	....	18.93	5.85	....	10.99	....
Sumter	7.71	7.18	8.40	....	....	....	....
Suwannee	2.24	....	1.92	....	5.34	....	....
Taylor	7.69	10.01	....	11.06	....	....	....
Union	4.19	4.69	....	....	....	....	....
Volusia	11.87	....	38.26	21.92	19.74	....	....
Wakulla	3.99	....	....	....	....	....	....
Walton	7.45	5.00	....	89.46	....	....	....
Washington	4.63	2.76	6.72	....	....	....	....
Highest	$55.33	$26.83	$38.26	$89.46	$63.22	$26.83	$27.11
Q₁	12.81	14.86	18.93	24.95	....	....	....
Median	8.22	7.18	9.28	16.92	18.52	17.30	....
Q₃	4.63	4.49	5.33	12.45	....	....	....
Lowest	1.60	1.56	1.51	5.85	5.34	10.99	14.88
Number of Cases	60	43	36	21	15	6	2

nomic power [6] used for public schools (shown in Table 15). That group of counties having the lowest average of wealth expends far more effort to produce the small amount of money which it spends; while, on the other hand, that group having the greatest average wealth expends far less effort and produces larger amounts of money. A larger taxing unit, such as the state, would tend to equalize the effort.[7, 8]

[6] Norton, J. K., *Ability of States to Support Education*, pp. 48-55.

[7] Mort, Paul R., *State Support of Public Schools*, pp. 35-38.

[8] Strayer, G. D. and Haig, R. M., *The Financing of Education in the State of New York*, p. 166.

It will be admitted that a county with a high ratio of adults to children has more earning capacity than one in which the ratio is low. The correlation between this measure and index of wealth for Florida counties is .55 ± .07. The relationship sug-

TABLE 14

TRUE WEALTH OF COUNTIES OF FLORIDA COMPARED WITH CURRENT EXPENSE COSTS PER PUPIL—WHITE AND NEGRO—1926–1927

COUNTIES RANKED BY TRUE WEALTH	TRUE WEALTH PER PUPIL	CURRENT EXPENSE PER PUPIL	
		White	Negro
First Group	$9,480–$27,581	$111.37	$29.00
Second Group	5,584– 9,272	76.07	20.10
Third Group	3,428– 5,073	60.21	11.44
Fourth Group	1,728– 3,224	45.01	5.91

gests that the two may be measures of the same thing. Clark [9] challenges the assumption that the relationship of ratio of adults to children in the population to ability is direct. Yet, since it is shown in Table 16 that the counties ranking high in other meas-

TABLE 15

PER CENT OF TOTAL ECONOMIC POWER EXPENDED FOR SCHOOLS FOR WHITES COMPARED WITH INDEX OF WEALTH AVERAGE FOR WHITE AND NEGRO

COUNTIES RANKED IN GROUPS	PER CENT OF ECONOMIC POWER FOR SCHOOLS	INDEX OF AVERAGE WEALTH
First Group	4.76%–13.67%	$1,677.00
Second Group	3.61 – 4.75	2,233.00
Third Group	2.86 – 3.50	1,631.00
Fourth Group	.30 – 2.71	3,523.00

ures of wealth also tend to rank high in this, the ratio is very conservative and is here used in the same way as are those other measures of wealth, such as "income" or true "valuation."

[9] Clark, Harold F., "The Effect of Population and Ability to Support Education," *Bulletin of the School of Education*, Indiana University, Vol. XI, No. 1.

The correlation between the ratio of adults to children and cost per pupil for current expense is .48 ± .07. If wealth is held constant the residual relationship for these two variables is .195. It can be said that varying ratios of adults to children in Florida tend to correspond with varying amounts of expenditures. That this condition may affect policies of the board which in turn cause variation may be deduced from the fact that there is a correlation of .799 ± .06 between this ratio and length of term. If counties with fewer children in their population have longer terms, ratio of adults to children is an external factor influencing educational policies.

TABLE 16

MEASURES OF WEALTH COMPARED WITH NUMBER OF DISTRICTS IN EACH COUNTY—WHITE

COUNTIES RANKED BY INDEX OF WEALTH	INDEX OF WEALTH PER PUPIL	NUMBER OF DISTRICTS
First Group	$4,319–$16,140	12.1
Second Group	2,720– 4,188	10.0
Third Group	1,651– 2,702	15.0
Fourth Group	339– 1,649	18.0

COUNTIES RANKED BY TRUE WEALTH	TRUE WEALTH PER PUPIL	NUMBER OF DISTRICTS
First Group	$9,480–$27,581	9.0
Second Group	5,584– 9,272	12.2
Third Group	3,428– 5,063	15.0
Fourth Group	1,728– 3,223	19.0

COUNTIES RANKED BY RATIO OF ADULTS TO CHILDREN	RATIO OF ADULTS TO CHILDREN	NUMBER OF DISTRICTS
First Group	1.43–2.55	12.7
Second Group	1.12–1.43	15.3
Third Group	.95–1.12	13.7
Fourth Group	.33– .94	19.9

DIVISIONS OF DISTRICTS

Wealthy counties not only spend more with less effort but are less handicapped by political divisions within the county. Table 16 shows that the wealthy counties, measured by index of wealth, true wealth, and ratio of adults to population, have fewer special tax districts than the less wealthy counties. Their resources are greater and at the same time more centralized. If counties of Florida could be organized as one unit, this handicap for the poorer counties would be overcome and much of the inequality of educational opportunity would be corrected. The county divided into many taxing districts, each administering its own school system, finds its financial ability greatly depleted.

Staffelbach,[10] in his study of the states, found that density of population affects cost per pupil. This principle probably holds good among the counties of Florida.

Table 17 shows that schools in counties having sparse population tend to be more costly than those in counties which are densely populated. The exception to this tendency is in the counties having extreme density. It would be logical to conclude that these counties spend more because of additional opportunity. Sears and Cubberley state in this connection:

When a school population has increased to the point where each organization unit, that is each classroom, is carrying a maximum load, and when the number of such units has increased to the point where each principal

TABLE 17

DENSITY OF POPULATION OF FLORIDA COUNTIES COMPARED WITH COST PER PUPIL FOR CURRENT EXPENSE—WHITE—1926–1927

COUNTIES RANKED BY TOTAL POPULATION PER SQUARE MILE	TOTAL POPULATION PER SQUARE MILE	COST PER WHITE PUPIL FOR CURRENT EXPENSE
First Group	26.2–176.4	$81.03
Second Group	15.2– 23.6	65.56
Third Group	9.3– 15.1	59.55
Fourth Group	0.2– 9.2	83.72

[10] Staffelbach, Elmer H., "The Relation of School Population Density to Educational Unit Costs in the States." *Educational Administration and Supervision*, Vol. XIV, No. 2, pp. 73-85.

and supervisor is carrying a maximum load, the system will then have reached the lowest per-pupil cost of output.[11]

In general, the larger the school, the more nearly it approximates these maxima. As one approaches these maxima in practice, however, another factor enters, viz., an increase in the quality of instruction provided. With increase in quality, cost tends to increase and tends to prevent the per-pupil cost from going down as normally would be the case in moving from small to large schools. It is almost certain that the increase in quality accounts for most of the gradual rise of the city school curve, that is, the downward pull of larger class groups is more than offset by the upward pull of more and better instruction.

URBANIZATION

Counties in which the larger cities of Florida are located tend to spend more per pupil than those counties in which there is no large center. The average cost for counties with urban centers is $86.87 per pupil for whites and $27.01 per pupil for Negroes (Table 18). The average for rural counties is $74.76 for each white child and $15.05 per child for Negroes. The probable error of the difference of these means for whites is 7.08; it is 3.6 for Negroes.

TABLE 18

COMPARISON OF AVERAGE EXPENDITURES FOR CURRENT EXPENSE, COUNTIES HAVING URBAN CENTERS AND RURAL COUNTIES—FLORIDA, 1926–1927

COUNTY	AVERAGE OBTAINED		STANDARD ERROR OF OBTAINED AVERAGE		DIFFERENCE OF AVERAGES URBAN RURAL		PROBABLE ERROR OF DIFFERENCE		CRITICAL RATIO DIFF. P.E.	
	White	Negro	White	Negro	White	Negro	White	Negro	White	Negro
Urban .	$86.87	$27.01	9.012	5.029	$12.11	$11.96	7.08	3.60	1.7	3.3
Rural ..	74.46	15.05	5.40	1.778						

The critical ratio for current expense for white children is 1.7.[12] It is 3.3 for Negroes. The difference is not real or significant for white children. Even this ratio, however, lends support to the idea that urbanization tends to increase school expenditures. It may be concluded from the critical ratio shown in Table 16 for Negroes, that they are more adequately provided for if they live near cities.

[11] Sears and Cubberley, *The Cost of Education in California*, pp. 161–62.
[12] McGaughy, James R., *The Fiscal Administration of City School Systems*, p. 71.

PUPIL POPULATION OF COUNTY

White Pupil Population. It is possible for counties having a larger number of pupils, other things being equal, to group their children more conveniently in centers. This should result in economy of expenditures, since more pupils can be assigned to one teacher and supplies can be purchased more economically. This should be true even when the county is divided into districts, since, by chance, the children would group more or less in centers within the county. Yet, when counties are grouped according to the number of pupils in average daily attendance, there is a distinct tendency for the current expense to be as high in the larger counties as in the smaller ones. This might be expected since congested districts are usually wealthier.

Counties with an average daily attendance above 4,000 expend four times as much per pupil for general control service as counties having an average daily attendance of 2,000 to 3,000. Counties having less than 1,000 pupils spend more per pupil than those with 2,000 to 3,000. So far as Florida is concerned, it seems that for general control the counties having 2,000 to 3,000 pupils are most economical.

For instructional service, all the counties tend to spend similar amounts. At least, there is no distinct tendency for large counties to spend more per pupil than small ones.

The trend is in the direction of larger counties spending more for operation and maintenance. The greatest variation in amount spent for these purposes occurs in the smaller counties where less is spent. No evidence is presented here, but it may be safely assumed that teachers do the janitor's work, that little heat is necessary, and that no repair work was needed in those counties during the year 1926-27.

Expenditures for auxiliary agencies show a different trend. The counties having few pupils spend more per pupil than do the counties with a large number of pupils. Here also, there is greater variation among the counties with a smaller school population. The range among groups is from $35.70 for counties with small school population to $14.52 for counties with more pupils.

Two causes operate to produce this effect:

TABLE 19

PER-PUPIL EXPENDITURES FOR ELEMENTARY AND HIGH SCHOOLS COMBINED, FOR WHITES, BY FUNCTIONS, FOR COUNTIES CLASSIFIED BY AVERAGE DAILY ATTENDANCE—FLORIDA, 1926–1927

Based on unpublished figures from the Office of State Superintendent of Public Instruction

AVERAGE DAILY ATTENDANCE	NUMBER OF CASES	GENERAL CONTROL	INSTRUCTIONAL SERVICE	OPERATION OF PLANT	MAINTENANCE OF PLANT	AUXILIARY AGENCIES	FIXED CHARGES	TOTAL CURRENT EXPENSES	REPAYMENTS OF BORROWED MONEY	INTEREST	TOTAL DEBT SERVICE	CAPITAL OUTLAY	GRAND TOTAL
Over 4,000	9												
Highest		$97.65	$ 90.31	$ 7.75	$31.48	$ 4.52	$ 3.53	$150.54	$ 96.61	$31.59	$128.20	$196.06	$406.21
Median		17.24	60.55	3.42	5.49	3.36	1.49	94.23	17.43	23.67	33.72	127.47	280.67
Lowest		2.48	24.05	1.64	1.85	1.19	.87	51.16	4.93	6.94	6.94	7.56	75.91
3,000 to 4,000 ...	6												
Highest		$22.69	$59.82	$ 2.99	$ 5.23	$ 9.05	$ 1.37	$ 98.10	$136.03	$21.55	$146.17	$ 94.82	$228.77
Median		15.68	39.27	2.11	3.34	4.68	1.08	70.17	25.47	15.49	50.72	52.51	208.53
Lowest		4.91	25.36	.37	.76	2.81	.47	35.18	2.19	4.77	6.96	10.93	85.79
2,000 to 3,000 ...	11												
Highest		$21.08	$ 61.26	$ 3.32	$13.43	$16.49	$ 3.10	$117.60	$ 88.90	$27.98	$116.78	$165.18	$399.56
Median		6.41	36.57	1.17	2.10	5.36	.92	58.22	13.95	11.17	23.99	22.95	111.17
Lowest		1.61	17.86	.19	00.00	.50	.10	25.12	00.00	2.17	2.17	.98	28.31
1,000 to 2,000 ...	20												
Highest		$32.78	$130.61	$ 4.87	$ 9.11	$10.66	$ 2.22	$ 85.91	$ 85.91	$17.82	$ 98.42	$ 53.56	$201.30
Median		11.18	36.50	1.20	2.50	5.35	.65	64.26	17.74	6.46	22.65	16.22	126.32
Lowest		1.59	21.95	.16	.30	1.62	.22	00.00	00.00	00.00	00.00	00.00	47.18
Under 1,000	21												
Highest		$34.90	$ 72.06	$ 4.97	$21.89	$35.70	$ 3.60	$158.22	$ 80.14	$26.31	$ 91.82	$282.72	$422.58
Median		9.71	45.07	1.30	1.62	7.93	.82	64.35	20.87	3.47	26.80	7.44	95.06
Lowest		2.82	20.12	0.00	.43	.58	0.00	26.38	00.00	00.00	00.00	.38	31.84

TABLE 20

PER-PUPIL EXPENDITURES FOR ELEMENTARY AND HIGH SCHOOLS COMBINED, FOR NEGROES, BY FUNCTIONS, FOR COUNTIES CLASSIFIED BY AVERAGE DAILY ATTENDANCE—FLORIDA, 1926-1927

Based on unpublished figures from the Office of State Superintendent of Public Instruction

AVERAGE DAILY ATTENDANCE	NUMBER OF CASES	GENERAL CONTROL	INSTRUCTIONAL SERVICE	OPERATION OF PLANT	MAINTENANCE OF PLANT	AUXILIARY AGENTS	FIXED CHARGES	TOTAL CURRENT EXPENSES	REPAYMENTS OF BORROWED MONEY	INTEREST	TOTAL DEBT SERVICE	CAPITAL OUTLAY	GRAND TOTAL
2,600 to 7,500 ...	6												
Highest		$42.83	$35.62	$2.13	$11.99	$00.00	$2.15	$93.00	$42.38	$13.85	$56.23	$27.41	$176.64
Median		2.23	14.98	.54	.77	00.00	.12	18.84	2.54	1.99	3.83	1.67	23.20
Lowest		.25	3.34	0.00	00.00	00.00	.01	3.69	0.00	.33	1.34	0.00	6.01
1,854 to 2,599 ...	9												
Highest		$ 6.65	$19.70	$ .99	$ 9.48	$00.00	$ .77	$31.32	$16.92	$ 4.81	$18.18	$24.07	$ 56.71
Median		1.08	15.45	.10	.06	00.00	.13	16.73	.98	1.42	2.96	.57	27.84
Lowest		.19	2.16	.00	0.00	00.00	.00	2.43	0.00	.06	.50	0.00	3.48
500 to 1,500 ...	18												
Highest		$26.12	$22.24	$ .85	$10.09	$ .41	$ .72	$51.80	$12.47	$ 6.94	$15.69	$48.84	$ 84.93
Median		1.12	8.69	.00	.18	.00	.03	10.13	3.64	1.39	5.89	.05	19.67
Lowest		.07	2.71	.00	0.00	.00	.00	3.19	0.00	.00	.67	.00	4.19
300 to 500 ...	15												
Highest		$22.81	$30.62	$ 2.41	$ 3.60	$ 3.85	$ 1.17	$44.12	$18.47	$13.28	$25.09	$79.63	$131.47
Median		1.73	12.70	0.00	.03	0.00	0.00	13.74	2.73	1.41	4.33	0.00	17.01
Lowest		.26	3.30	0.00	0.00	0.00	0.00	3.56	0.00	.30	.30	0.00	5.09
Less than 300 ...	19												
Highest		$ 3.55	$30.90	$ 0.00	$ 0.00	$ 0.00	$ 0.00	$32.20	$ 7.66	$ 3.79	$ 8.68	$00.00	$ 35.30
Median		.87	6.68	0.00	0.00	0.00	0.00	8.62	.84	.38	2.06	00.00	10.01
Lowest				0.00	0.00	0.00	0.00	0.00	0.00	0.00	0.00	00.00	00.00

1. The counties having fewer pupils pay a large part of their current expense for transportation purposes, which constitute the major part of expenditures for auxiliary agencies.
2. The counties having fewer pupils also vary in the provision for transportation because of the fact that they have less wealth with which to provide the service.

There is little difference among groups of counties classified by number of pupils, in the amount spent for fixed charges. This is probably due to the fact that counties with many pupils carry more insurance while counties with fewer pupils pay more for rent. There is no definite policy within any group of counties as to methods of handling problems of insurance and rent. Conditions are met as they arise and the solution varies as to time, place, and personnel.

Table 19 indicates that there is no definite policy or standard with respect to the amount paid for debt service which is in any way dependent upon the size of county. Large or small counties tend to spend a large proportion of their current expenditures for debt service.

Negro Pupil Population. Those counties which have the largest numbers of Negro children in average daily attendance tend to spend more per pupil for total current expense, as shown in Table 20. When total current expense is divided into instructional and noninstructional costs, both are shown to increase as the size of the county increases. From these comparisons, it may be said that the Negro school population of the county has slightly less effect on the amount spent per Negro pupil for debt service. The Negro school population for the county seems to be closely related to variation in current expenditures in Negro schools. In other words, if Negro children are provided with any educational opportunity, the tendency is to improve quality as the numbers increase.

CHAPTER IV

SUMMARY AND CONCLUSIONS

The variation in the amount spent per pupil among counties of Florida is even more extreme than that disclosed in other studies. Each function of the distribution discloses this tendency toward wide differences in per-pupil expenditures.

The conditions which are related to variation among Florida counties are of two general types. The internal factors, or those over which a board of education exercises control, will of necessity cause differences in amount spent per pupil as the policies respecting them differ. The policies of the board of education, however, are determined under the influence of external conditions or conditions over which it can exercise no control. Any difference in these conditions causes differences in policies of boards.

The internal and external factors and conditions considered in this study are classified here according to their degree of importance when related to variation. Those conditions which affect variation in counties of Florida to a considerable extent are classified as more important. Those having less influence are classified as less important. Since some factors have different effects upon expenditures for Negro schools than they have for white schools, they are listed separately by races.

CONDITIONS WITHIN THE SCHOOL SYSTEM WHICH ARE RELATED TO THE AMOUNT OF EXPENDITURES

White Schools

More Important

1. Length of term.

2. Number of teachers in a school.

3. Amount paid per pupil for debt service.

Less Important

1. In large schools—the size of class.

2. Per cent of pupils in a county who are transported.

3. Per cent of indebtedness based on true wealth.

48

4. The average amount paid for
capital outlay.
5. In small classes or one-teacher
schools—the size of class.

White Schools

More important

1. Wealth.
   a. True value of taxable property.
   b. Index of wealth.
      (1) Business ratings of county.
   c. Ratio of adults to children.
2. Type of population.
   Per cent of population coming
   from other than southern states.
3. Per cent of economic power which
   is devoted to education.
4. Number of districts into which a
   county is divided.
5. Density of population.

Less important

1. Urbanization.

2. Number of white pupils in average daily attendance within the
   county.
3. Type of population.
   a. Per cent of incoming popula-
      tion from southern states.
   b. Per cent Negro population is
      of total population.

The variation is wider among Negro schools than it is among white. Negro schools in Florida are dependent, more or less, upon the attitude of boards of education toward Negro education. There is no way by which this attitude can be measured except to say that as more Negro children are kept in school there tends to be less variation in current expense per pupil. Since counties with more Negro pupils in average daily attendance spend more per pupil for education, it may be said that, as the Negro population increases, the counties tend to provide more adequately for this education.

As was stated above, some factors and conditions have a different effect on Negro schools than they have upon white schools. Whereas a white teacher who is employed in a large school may expect to have more pupils and receive a higher salary, the Negro teacher who teaches in a large school may expect to have more pupils and receive less pay. For factors which affect both, the general tendency is for them to have greater influence upon the Negro schools than upon the white. On the whole, however, it may be said that methods of control of expenditures may be set up through internal factors for both races.

CONDITIONS WITHIN THE SCHOOL SYSTEM WHICH ARE RELATED TO THE
AMOUNT OF EXPENDITURES*

Negro Schools

More important

1. Length of term.
2. Number of teachers in a school.
3. Amount paid per pupil for debt service.
4. Average amount paid for capital outlay.
5. Size of class.

Less important

1. Per cent of indebtedness based upon true wealth.

CONDITIONS OUTSIDE THE SCHOOL SYSTEM WHICH ARE RELATED TO THE
AMOUNT OF EXPENDITURE OVER WHICH A BOARD EXERCISES NO CONTROL

Negro Schools

More important

1. Wealth.
   a. True value of taxable property.
   b. Index of wealth.
      (1) Business ratings of county.
   c. Ratio of adults to children.
2. Type of population.
   Per cent of population coming from other than southern states.
3. Per cent of economic power which is devoted to education.
4. Density of population.
5. Number of negro pupils in average daily attendance within a county.
6. Urbanization.

Less important

1. Type of population.

2. Per cent Negro population is of total population.

* These are listed in the order of their importance.

The length of term for either race may be adjusted uniformly. The size of school, when measured by number of teachers or number of pupils, can be adjusted to sizes compatible with economy and efficiency. These adjustments would reduce variation in cost per pupil. Since a board of education cannot control external conditions directly, the adjustment suggested must be made according to these conditions as they are.

The best method of adjusting conditions for equalization purposes has been worked out by Professor Paul R. Mort and by his students in other states.[1, 2, 3] This plan establishes the minimum

[1] Mort, Paul R., *State Support for Public Schools.*

[2] Morrison, Fred Wilson, *Equalization of the Financial Burden of Education in North Carolina.*

[3] Singleton, Gordon G., *State Responsibility for the Support of Education in Georgia.*

amount which should be expended by any community on the basis of the average educational expenditures of the communities of average wealth of the state. Every community is required to tax itself uniformly to support the educational program imposed by the State. Such uniformity is determined as a tax rate based upon equalized valuation, no higher than that necessary in the ablest community. In this way, wealthier districts contribute to the educational opportunity offered to children in less fortunate districts.

BIBLIOGRAPHY

SPECIFIC REFERENCES

AYRES, LEONARD P. *An Index for State School Systems.* Russell Sage Foundation, 1920. 70 pp.

ENGELHARDT, FRED and VON BORGERSRODE, FRED. *Accounting Procedure for School Systems.* Bureau of Publications, Teachers College, Columbia University, 1927. 130 pp.

HENRY, NELSON B. *A Study of Public School Costs in Illinois Cities.* Educational Finance Inquiry. New York. Macmillan Company, 1924. 82 pp.

HUNT, CHARLES W. *The Cost and Support of Secondary Schools in the State of New York.* Educational Finance Inquiry. New York: Macmillan Company, 1924. 107 pp.

McGAUGHY, JAMES R. *Fiscal Administration of City School Systems.* Educational Finance Inquiry. New York: Macmillan Company, 1924. 94 pp.

MORRISON, FRED WILSON.. *Equalization of the Financial Burden of Education in North Carolina.* Bureau of Publications, Teachers College, Columbia University, 1925.

MORRISON, HENRY C. *The Financing of Public Schools in the State of Illinois.* Educational Finance Inquiry. New York: Macmillan Company, 1924. 162 pp.

MORT, PAUL R. *State Support for Public Schools.* Bureau of Publications, Teachers College, Columbia University, 1926.

NORTON, JOHN KELLEY. *Education and the Federal Government.* National Educational Association, 1926. 88 pp.

REEVES, FLOYD W. *The Political Unit of Public School Finance in Illinois;* Educational Finance Inquiry. Macmillan Company, 1924. 166 pp.

RUSSELL, WILLIAM F., HOLY, THOMAS C., STONE, RALEIGH W., and OTHERS. *The Financing of Education in Iowa.* Educational Finance Inquiry. New York: Macmillan Company, 1925. 279 pp.

SEARS, JESSE B. and CUBBERLEY, ELLWOOD P. *The Cost of Education in California.* Educational Finance Inquiry. New York: Macmillan Company, 1924. 351 pages.

STEEP, R. O. *Elementary School Costs in the State of New York.* Educational Finance Inquiry. New York: Macmillan Company, 1924. 123 pp.

STRAYER, GEORGE D. *City School Expenditures.* Teachers College, Columbia University, 1905. 104 pp.

SINGLETON, GORDON G. *State Responsibility for the Support of Education in Georgia.* Bureau of Publications, Teachers College, Columbia University. 1925. 56 pp.

STRAYER, GEORGE D. and HAIG, ROBERT MURRAY. *The Financing of Education in the State of New York.* Educational Finance Inquiry. New York: 1923. 205 pp.

STRAYER, GEORGE D. *Report of the Survey of the Schools of Lynn, Massachusetts,* Chap. 3, pp. 118-148. The Institute of Educational Research, Division of Field Studies, Teachers College, Columbia University. Bureau of Publications, Teachers College, Columbia University, 1927. 368 pp.

STRAYER, GEORGE D. and ENGELHARDT, N. L. *Report of the Survey of the Schools of Port Arthur, Texas.* Port Arthur Educational Commission, Bureau of Publications, Teachers College, Columbia University.

SWIFT, FLETCHER H. *The Public School System of Arkansas.* Public School Finance, Part II, 1923, No. 11; Washington Government Printing Office. 107 pp.

THOMAS, FRANK W. *Training for Effective Study.* Riverside Textbooks in Education; E. P. Cubberley, Editor. Houghton Mifflin Company, 1922.

WILLETT, GEORGE W. *The Public School Debt.* Educational Finance Inquiry. Macmillan Company, 1924. 97 pp.

GENERAL REFERENCES

ENGELHARDT, N. L. and ENGELHARDT, FRED. *Public School Finance.* Bureau of Publications, Teachers College, Columbia University, 1927. 1068 pp.

LUTZ, HARLEY FEIST. *Public Finance.* New York: D. Appleton & Company, 1927. 681 pp.

McGAUGHY, JAMES R. *Teachers' Salaries in New York City.* Bureau of Publications, Teachers College, Columbia University, 1927. 256 pp.

MOEHLMAN, ARTHUR B. *Public School Finance.* New York: Rand McNally and Company, 1927. 508 pp.

MORT, PAUL R. *State Support for Public Schools.* Bureau of Publications, Teachers College, Columbia University, 1926. 104 pp.

STRAYER, ENGELHARDT, and OTHERS. *Problems in Educational Administration;* Problem 18, pp. 159-163. Bureau of Publications, Teachers College, Columbia University, 1925. 755 pp.

BULLETINS

SPECIFIC REFERENCES

CLARK, HAROLD F. "The Effect of Population Upon Ability to Support Education." *Bulletin of the Bureau of Coöperative Research,* Vol. II, No. 1. University of Indiana, 28 pp.

HARRIS, W. T. "Conditions Which Cause Variation in the Rate of School Expenditures." *Proceedings of Department of Superitendence,* National Education Assocation, Milwaukee, Wisconsin, 1905. 63 pp.

"Some Accompaniments of the Differences in Ability to Support Education and the Permanency of These Differences." *Research Bulletin of the National Education Association,* pp. 39-60.

"Facts on the Cost of Public Education." *Research Bulletin of National Education Association,* Vol. I, No. 1, 4-8, pp. 16 and 63, June, 1922.

STAFFELBACH, ELMER H. "The Relationship of School Population Density to Educational Unit-Costs in the States." *Educational Administration and Supervision including Teacher Training,* Utah, Bul. 18, 1926; February, 1928, pp. 73-85.

GENERAL REFERENCES

"Why School Costs Appear Burdensome." *Research Bulletin of National Education Association,* Vol. I, No. 2, March, 1923; pp. 78-82.

"Do Good Schools Pay?" *Research Bulletin of the National Education Association,* Vol. I, No. 4, September, 1923, pp. 299-306.

"Progress in Securing Adequate School Support." *Research Bulletin of the National Education Association,* Vol. V, No. 4, September, 1927, pp. 216-221.

"School Costs and Economic Resources of the Various States." *Research Bulletin of the National Education Association,* Vol. 7, No. 1, January, 1927, pp. 7-29.

"State Advance toward Sound School Finance Program." *Research Bulletin of the National Education Association,* Vol. 7, No. 1, January, 1927, pp. 30-37.